I love
TENNIS

In association with the
WIMBLEDON JUNIOR TENNIS INITIATIVE

DK

LONDON, NEW YORK, MUNICH,
MELBOURNE, AND DELHI

Senior Designer Lisa Lanzarini
Designer Rebecca Johns
Project Editor Lindsay Fernandes
Editor Kate Simkins
Consultant Dan Bloxham
Publishing Manager Cynthia O'Neill Collins
Art Director Mark Richards
Category Publisher Alex Kirkham
Production Claire Pearson
DTP Dean Scholey

First American Edition, 2005
Published in the United States by
DK Publishing, Inc., 375 Hudson Street,
New York, New York 10014

05 06 07 08 09 10 9 8 7 6 5 4 3 2 1

Copyright © 2004 Dorling Kindersley Limited
All images © Dorling Kindersley Limited
For further information see: www.dkimages.com

A Cataloging-in-Publication record for this book is available from the
Library of Congress.

ISBN 0-7566-0309-9

Reproduced by Colourscan, Singapore
Printed and bound in Slovakia by Tlaciarne BB

Discover more at
www.dk.com

I love TENNIS

In association with the

WIMBLEDON JUNIOR TENNIS INITIATIVE

Written by Naia Bray-Moffatt

Contents

Introduction

Tennis is a game for everyone.
You can play it just for fun with
your friends, or enjoy the thrill of
taking part in competitions.
You will have learned a skill for life.
Give it a try and play!

Maria loves coming to tennis school. She has made lots of new friends.

Who's Who

Maria, Helen, and Ida have just joined the tennis school, and they are having a great time. Nathan, Chloé, Samuel, and Alisha have been playing a bit longer and have learned lots of skills. All the children are happy to be playing such a fun sport.

Nathan

Helen

Maria

Nathan likes to hit the forehand.

Helen is trying out volleying.

Maria wants to learn how to serve.

Ida likes to play on the clay court.

Chloé is very athletic and fast.

Samuel has a great backhand.

Alisha (left) is also at the tennis school. She enjoys playing matches. Elizabeth (right) is twelve years old and has been playing for a few years. Sometimes she helps the younger children with their tennis practice.

Ida

Chloé

Samuel

Dan is a qualified tennis coach and has a special license to teach children how to play. He loves showing them how much fun tennis can be.

Getting Started

Maria is six, and she has just started taking tennis lessons at the tennis courts in her city park. The tennis coach has rackets and balls for the children in the class to practice with, so Maria doesn't need to bring much to start with. The most important things she needs are well-fitting tennis shoes, comfortable clothes for running around in, and lots of energy!

Tennis clothes

Tennis can be played indoors or outdoors, but either way, you will get pretty hot from running around, so it's a good idea to wear loose-fitting and lightweight clothes. Tennis shoes should have rubber soles to help them grip and be cushioned to give your ankles support. Thick sports socks will help protect your feet from blisters. Traditionally, tennis clothes are white, but for practice, any color will do.

Alisha makes sure her hair is tied back off her face.

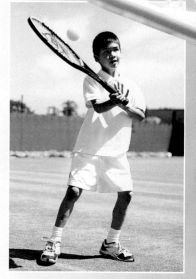

Wear a hat and sunscreen when you're playing outdoors in the sun, and always have lots to drink.

Helen wears shorts and a top, but a tennis dress or skirt and top can be worn, too.

Samuel's shorts have pockets that are useful for keeping a spare ball in.

Maria learns what it feels like to hold a tennis racket and is surprised by how light it is.

Tennis rackets

Most tennis schools will have rackets that you can borrow until you decide that you want to buy one of your own. They come in different sizes, and it's important to choose one that is comfortable to hold and the right size for you.

Tennis balls

Foam tennis balls like the red one are sometimes used when you first start learning to play. They are soft and have a slow bounce, which makes them easier to hit. After a while, you may play with orange-and-yellow balls (transition balls), which bounce slightly faster than foam balls. Later on, you will use standard yellow tennis balls. They are made of rubber and have a fast bounce.

11

Warming Up

Maria keeps her arms stretched out to the side to help her balance, while she concentrates on tapping a tennis ball with her toes.

Tennis lessons always begin with a warm-up routine. This means doing different exercises to make sure that all the muscles in your body are warmed up and ready before you start playing the game. This is important because otherwise you could hurt yourself. Dan makes sure the exercises are fun to do and help with concentration, too.

Jogging in place

Jumping

Jogging and jumping

You need to be able to move your feet quickly when you play tennis. Jogging and jumping in place are good exercises for helping to warm up your feet and leg muscles. You can practice these exercises anywhere. Try to be light on your feet. It is also important to do exercises to warm up your arms.

Circling your arms in the air like windmills while jumping stretches all your muscles.

12

Stretching

Stretching exercises help loosen up your muscles and can be done even while you're standing still. Stand with your feet apart, hands on your hips, and move from side to side to stretch your tummy and waist muscles.

Crocodile steps

The children follow Dan along the lines of the tennis court to help improve their balance. They pretend that if they fall off the lines, the crocodiles will come and snap them up!

Nathan likes throwing and catching a ball best. To begin with, he throws the ball underhand. It is more difficult to throw it overhand.

Ball Skills

Dan now brings out the tennis balls for the next part of the lesson. Learning basic ball skills, such as bouncing and catching a ball and throwing and rolling a ball, are some of the most important skills you can learn as a tennis player. That is why all tennis players spend a lot of time practicing them. At tennis school, the children try out some ball skills on their own and other skills in a group.

Rolling the ball

Placing the ball

It's easy to roll a ball, but to make the ball go exactly where you want it to takes a bit of practice. Dan shows the girls how to make their hands follow through in the right direction before letting go of the ball.

Come on, girls! You can do it!

Who is Dan going to roll the ball to next? The girls have to pay attention and be ready to bend down and trap the ball in their hands if it's rolling their way.

Keep it rolling

Now the girls roll the ball to each other. They are learning how to play together as a team.

Ida and Helen try out different ways of rolling the ball to each other. They use different hands to roll the ball and try rolling it to the left and then to the right. Sometimes they roll the ball slowly and sometimes quickly.

14

Bounce, catch

Bouncing and catching a ball by yourself is a good way of helping you to "judge" the ball. The harder you bounce it, the faster the ball will come back to you. Be ready to catch it! Try saying the words "bounce" and "catch" out loud to yourself as you do it.

Ida is bouncing and catching the ball. She watches the ball closely and catches it firmly with both hands.

"I had to really stretch to catch the ball, but I did it!**"**
Ida

Good work, Ida! She has had to run fast to catch the ball that Dan has thrown her. She has even caught it with one hand!

Run, bounce, and catch

Running to catch a ball after it bounces teaches you to be quick on your feet and to focus on the ball. Sometimes Dan throws a ball that bounces short, and the children have to run fast to catch it. If he throws a longer ball, they have more time.

15

Racket Skills

Maria has almost forgotten that to play tennis, you need a tennis racket! This is what makes tennis different from many other ball games. Before the class starts to hit the ball, they need to get used to holding the racket. They also need to be familiar with how the ball and racket feel together. Learning how to control the ball and feeling comfortable with your racket are important skills.

Tightrope walking

Ida is excited to be using a racket for the first time.

Maria is concentrating hard to make sure the ball stays on the racket as she weaves around the cones.

Balancing the ball on their racket heads, Ida and Maria imagine the court line they are walking along is a tightrope. They have to keep the ball steady as they walk carefully along the line.

Racket rolling

Using your tennis racket to roll the ball to a partner isn't quite as easy as using your hands. Maria and Helen concentrate on swinging the racket at the same time as watching the ball. In this exercise, they are taking the first step to playing a real game of tennis.

Maria stands in an open-stance position, but she turns her shoulders to hit the ball rolling toward her.

The girls listen to the sound the ball makes when it is dropped in the middle of the racket head. This is the area you want to hit the ball. It is called the sweet spot. When you hit the ball there, it makes a loud "ping" sound.

Playing "ping"

Walking the ball

In this exercise, the class has to walk around the cones without letting the ball fall off the racket. You need a steady hand!

17

Starting to Hit

Now it's time for the class to use their rackets to hit the ball. There are a lot of different ways to hit the ball. These are called strokes, and the class will learn them later on. To begin with, though, Dan wants the children simply to take a swing. It doesn't matter how they do it. If they manage to hit the ball and get it over the net, they are doing really well.

Are you ready to hit the ball?

The first thing Dan shows the class is the ready position. This is how you stand when you're waiting to hit the ball, to give you the best chance of returning it (hitting it back). Stand with your legs shoulder-width apart and knees slightly bent. Hold your racket with both hands in front of you.

Wherever the ball bounces, Maria is ready for it. She can easily move her racket to either side, and her slightly bent knees mean she's ready to run.

Working with the coach

Dan makes it easier for the class to hit the ball back to him by letting the children stand quite close to the net. As they improve, they will be able to hit the ball standing farther back from the net.

Ida hits a high ball before it bounces and gets it over the net. Then she turns her body to hit the next ball on her left.

Hit or miss!

Don't worry if you find it hard to hit the ball at first. It takes a lot of practice and concentration. Even top players sometimes miss the ball or hit it into the net. Keep trying.

" *I missed the first few balls, but then I hit one!* **"**

Helen

Court surfaces

Tennis can be played on tennis courts with different surfaces. A grass tennis court will make the ball have a skidding bounce that is low and fast. A hard court gives the ball a medium bounce. Clay courts have a powdery surface that makes the ball bounce slower.

Grass court

Nathan and Samuel play a fast game on a grass court.

Clay court

Helen enjoys having more time to hit the ball on clay courts.

Hard court

Maria likes the hard court because the ball doesn't skid.

Joining the Squad

Nathan, Samuel, Alisha and Chloé love being in the squad. Playing so much tennis together has made them great friends.

Going to tennis school is such fun that once a week is not enough for some children. The children who join the squad have lessons four times a week and play after school and on weekends. Maria, Helen, and Ida are thrilled to join the squad and look forward to learning more skills and working to improve their game.

Crossover steps

You need to be quick on your feet when you're playing tennis, and this crossover exercise is a good one for improving your footwork, as well as testing your balance and coordination.

| *Start the crossover steps* | *Cross over to the left* | *Uncross* |

1 To begin, stand with your feet slightly apart on the baseline, your knees bent, and your arms stretched out to the side.

2 Next, raise your right leg and bring it over your left leg so that your legs are crossed. You will have moved to the left.

3 Now uncross your legs by stepping to the left with your left leg. You will then be standing with your feet apart once again.

Power skipping

Energy, power, and control are all needed in tennis. Nathan finds the power to lift his knees as high as he can in this skipping exercise. He keeps his head still and controls the movement to make sure he skips on the line and stays balanced.

The new members of the squad look at a tennis book for some handy tips.

" *Tennis stretches me in lots of ways!* **"**

Nathan

4 Bring your right leg behind your left leg. Then take a step to the side with your left leg so that your feet are apart again. Keep going until you gct to the end of the line.

Warming up the ball

Dan and Alisha demonstrate some more advanced ball skills in an exercise they call "warming up the ball." Dan throws the ball to Alisha, who catches it in one hand, passes it to the other hand and throws it back to Dan. Then Dan introduces a second ball, and they do the same thing with two balls! This teaches you how to do one thing while thinking about another.

Hitting Skills

Things are picking up now. All the children feel confident holding a racket. They have enjoyed trying to hit the ball over the net. Dan thinks they are now ready to try some techniques to help them hit the ball with more power and accuracy. In this lesson, they will learn different ways of holding the racket to hit different strokes.

Holding the racket
The girls all now have rackets of their own. They are proud of their rackets and practice holding them. They put their strongest hand at the bottom of the handle, leaving enough room to place their other hand above it.

"*I love hitting the ball really hard.***"**

Nathan

22

Forehand grip

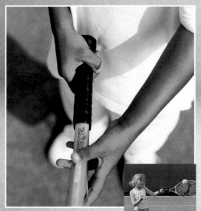

The V-shape between your index finger and thumb should be on the right-hand edge of the handle.

Backhand grip

For beginners, it is best to use two hands when hitting a backhand. Some players use one hand, but this is a bit trickier to do.

Continental grip

This is the grip for serving or volleying. The V-shape between your index finger and thumb should be to the left-hand edge of the top of the handle.

Grips

The way you hold the racket is called your racket grip. Tennis players learn to change their grip depending on the stroke they are going to use to hit the ball. To begin with, the most important grips to learn are the forehand and backhand grips.

These examples are for right-handed players. If you are left-handed, simply do the grips the opposite way around.

Serve and volley grip

Once you can do the forehand and backhand grips, you will learn the continental or serve and volley grip. Elizabeth is demonstrating this grip. It can be used to hit a forehand or backhand volley.

Elizabeth is one of the most experienced players in the squad. She is good at changing her grip for different strokes.

Forehand Drive

Bounce, hit! There are two groundstrokes in tennis, called the forehand drive and backhand drive, where you let the ball bounce once before you hit it. Today, the squad is going to practice the forehand drive, which for most people is the easiest to learn. Chloé, Nathan, and Samuel, who have been in the squad for longer, already have good forehand drives and are able to show the younger members how to do it.

Chloé is a left-handed player, but the rules for hitting the forehand are the same.

Low-to-high swing

To hit a forehand drive, you make a swinging action with your racket. Begin by taking your racket back in a low position. Then start to swing the racket up high enough to hit the ball so that it will go over the net. Keep swinging the racket up so that it ends up high above your shoulder.

Take-back	Swinging the racket	Hitting the ball	Follow-through

1 Nathan brings his racket back, turning his shoulders to the side.

2 Moving forward to meet the ball, Nathan swings his racket forward and upward.

3 Nathan hits the ball in front of his body. His weight is on his front foot.

4 Nathan continues the swing so that his racket arm reaches over his other shoulder.

Now Maria gives it a try. As she gets ready to swing, she uses her body weight to move toward the ball.

"Today, I started to hit the forehand. I love it!"

Helen

Foot position

Getting your feet in the correct position for each stroke will help your balance so that you are able to hit the ball more easily. For the forehand drive, move your feet so that you are standing sideways on to the ball and bend your knees.

Helen concentrates really hard on swinging her racket back, ready to hit the ball in the middle of her racket.

What a swing!

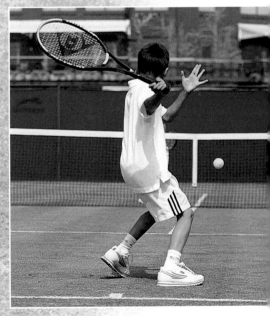

Samuel is standing near the baseline, right at the back of the court. He has to hit the ball really hard to make sure it will go over the net. The bigger the swing, the farther the ball will travel.

Backhand Drive

The older members of the squad are now going to practice the other groundstroke: the backhand drive. This is the stroke you use to hit the ball when it bounces on the side opposite your racket arm. When you first start learning it, you will probably use two hands. A double-handed backhand gives you strength and power. You may find the backhand difficult to learn at first, but with practice, it becomes a powerful stroke.

Maria has not started to learn the backhand drive yet. She watches to see how the others do it.

Two-handed backhand

The backhand drive, like the forehand, is a swinging stroke that starts off low and ends up high. Remember to change your grip as you turn to the side and to keep both hands on the handle.

Swing that racket back

It's a hit!

Over the shoulder

1 Samuel turns his shoulders and feet to the side and brings back his racket with both hands as far as he can.

2 Samuel steps forward to meet the ball and swings his racket up. Wham! He hits the ball with all his strength.

3 Continuing the swing, Samuel follows through with his racket, bringing it up over his shoulder.

Left-handed backhand

Being left-handed means Chloé does everything the same as a right-handed player but in reverse. She holds the bottom of the racket handle with her left hand and uses her right hand for added strength above it. Some of today's best tennis players are left-handed.

Did it go over?

4   As Samuel watches the ball sail over the net, he starts to bring his feet back to the ready position for the next shot.

Way to go! Hitting the backhand with two hands gives Alisha confidence as well as strength.

"*The backhand is my favorite stroke.***"**

Alisha

27

The Volley

Ida stands with her feet apart and her knees bent to hit the volley.

The class comes up closer to the net and tries hitting the ball before it bounces. This shot is called the volley. There are low volleys and high volleys. You can hit them forehand or backhand, but the action is always the same: a short, sharp punch. There is less time to hit the ball before it bounces, so you need to have fast reactions.

Forehand volley

Unlike the forehand drive, you do not use a big swing to hit the forehand volley. There isn't enough time, since the speed of the ball before it bounces is faster. Raise your racket above the ball, then step forward and use your weight to punch the ball with the racket.

Maria gets the hang of volleying.

Because Helen is just learning how to volley, she uses the forehand grip to hold the racket. Later on, she will learn a special grip for hitting volleys.

Backhand volley

To hit the backhand volley, use two hands to give more strength to your punching action. Later on, you will learn to hit forehand and backhand volleys with one hand to give you more reach.

"*This is fun!*"

Maria

High volley

Samuel hits a high volley down over the net. This is his winning shot. He often uses it when playing a game to win a point.

Low volley

To hit this low volley, Samuel has to angle his racket so that the ball will be lifted over the net.

29

Learning to Serve

The service, or serve, is the most important stroke to learn in tennis because it begins every point in a game. It is also the hardest to learn because you have to throw the ball up with one hand while swinging the racket and hitting the ball with the other. Even top tennis players don't always get their first serve right, which is why you are allowed two tries.

The serve

The server stands just behind the baseline. If it's a singles game, you stand near the center mark and hit the serve diagonally over the net into the service box. If the ball hits the net but still goes over, you can take your first serve again. A second serve is usually slower because you must be careful not to make a mistake.

Prepare to serve   *Throw the ball up*   *Wait for it!*

Throwing the ball up straight and high takes lots of practice.

1   Samuel stands behind the baseline with his body turned sideways. He holds the ball out in front and takes the racket behind.

2   As Samuel brings his racket back and up, he lifts his ball arm above his head, releasing the ball at full stretch.

3   Samuel bends his racket arm, ready to hit the ball. He needs to strike it at the highest point he can reach.

Half-serve

When you have learned to serve correctly, the stroke will be one continuous movement. This takes lots of practice. At first, Dan starts Maria off with the half-serve. He shows her how to bring the racket behind her back first and then throw up the ball before hitting it.

And hit!

4 Samuel throws the racket over his head and hits the ball. He lets the racket keep swinging to the other side of his body.

Helen holds the ball at the end of her fingers and practices throwing it up in the air.

Returning the serve

This is the next most important shot! Stand in the ready position so you can move quickly to use forehand or backhand. You want to return the ball to a part of the court that is difficult for your opponent to get to.

Will it be a forehand or backhand? Nathan focuses hard on the ball so he can get to it as soon as possible. He keeps his back straight and his head up.

"Dan always tells us
we've done well when
we shake hands at
the end of a lesson."

Helen

Watch and Learn

The children have done really well in their lessons and have learned a lot of skills from practicing and playing. In today's lesson, they are going to learn some more skills by sitting down and watching someone else playing. Elizabeth is an older member of the squad and is able to perform some strokes that her younger friends haven't been taught yet.

The smash

This is a stroke you will learn when you are a more confident player. It is used to hit a high ball either before or after it has bounced—you may need to jump if it's a really high ball. The racket arm action is similar to hitting a serve. If hit successfully, a smash is difficult to return.

Ready to smash   *Lift off!*   *Land on your feet!*

1 *Elizabeth brings her racket behind her and stretches her other arm up. She bends her knees, ready to spring up toward the ball.*

2 *As she throws her racket up over her head, Elizabeth jumps to meet the ball. She stretches her whole body as high as she can to hit the shot.*

3 *Now Elizabeth follows through with her racket, swinging it to the other side of her body. She keeps her head up so she can watch the ball and make sure she has hit a winning shot.*

To be a good tennis player, you need to want to win. But it's also important to enjoy the game. Elizabeth loves it and practices whenever she can.

"I am very proud to be an example to my friends."

Elizabeth

The children watch Elizabeth hit a perfect double-handed backhand. She is a great role model for the other girls in the squad.

The girls talk about what they've learned in their lesson and discuss which game they want to play.

Playing Games

At the end of each lesson, the children are pretty tired, but they always have enough energy for playtime! Sometimes they play team games, and sometimes they play point-scoring games to learn about winning and losing. The games are always lots of fun. The children really enjoy playing them and practicing the skills they have learned in their lesson at the same time.

After the lesson, Dan asks the class questions about what they have learned. If they get the answers right, they can choose the next game to play.

Ring around the rosie

This is good for improving your footwork. The girls hold hands and sidestep in a circle around the ball. When Dan calls "change," they have to change directions without letting go of each other's hands.

Sleeping giant

Your ball control has to be really good to win this game. The children have to keep the ball on their racket while they creep up on Dan, the sleeping giant. If he wakes up and catches someone moving, or if the ball falls off the racket, they have to start over.

The giant's asleep but not for long...

Now, he's awake. Has he caught anyone out?

Playing a Match

Now that the children have learned the different tennis strokes, they are ready to play a match. The younger players play on smaller-sized courts and play shorter matches. Different rules and scoring are used when playing a match on a full-sized court. But in any kind of match, the most important things are to play your best and enjoy it. Good luck!

" *Thank you for playing!* **"**
Alisha

In a friendly match, it's up to the players to call whether a ball is in or out. The player closest to the ball should do this. A ball is in if it lands on or inside the court lines. It's important to be fair and honest about line-calling.

Fair play

Some rules of tennis are not written down but are just as important to learn. These concern your manners on court and how you behave. Play to win, but play fairly. Always thank your opponent at the end of a match.

Chloé concentrates hard on every stroke. She is determined to play her best and think positively.

Doubles

In a doubles game, you play with a partner. You should support and help each other and work together as a team. Never blame your partner if something goes wrong

At the end of a point, it's polite to pick up the balls and return them to the server for the next point.

39

A Mini-Tournament

Maria has come a long way since her first day at tennis school. Now, she proudly holds her certificate as a record of her achievements.

At the end of classes, the coach sets up a mini-tournament for all the children in the tennis school. The different age groups take turns playing matches against each other, watched by their families and friends, who are invited to come and cheer them on. It's a nice, sunny day, and the children enjoy showing everyone their newly learned skills.

Taking turns

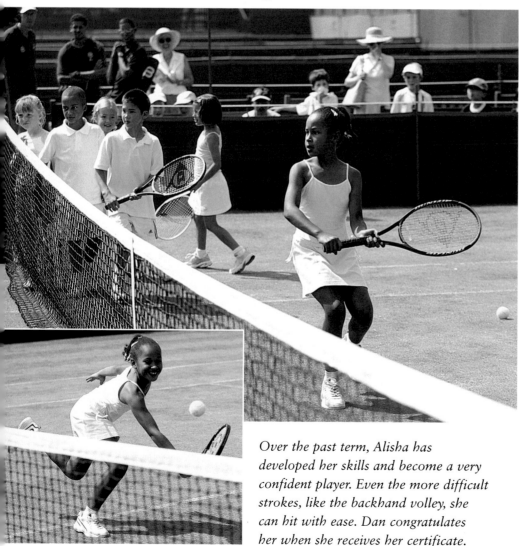

Warm-up games

Before the children start to play their matches, they play some games to warm up. They line up and, as Dan throws the ball to them, they run to hit backhand volleys. It's great fun. They soon forget to be nervous about playing in the mini-tournament.

Over the past term, Alisha has developed her skills and become a very confident player. Even the more difficult strokes, like the backhand volley, she can hit with ease. Dan congratulates her when she receives her certificate.

Spectators

Playing a match with their friends and families watching is the first time the children have played in front of an audience. It can give you confidence to hear the audience supporting you, and help you to play better—but it's important to keep your concentration.

Nathan and Samuel are evenly matched in their tennis skills. Today, Nathan won the match, but Samuel might win when they next play each other. They both proudly show their certificates.

Nathan tries to forget that he is playing against his best friend. He tries his hardest to win.

Playing at Wimbledon

A few people have already taken their seats at the edge of the court where the junior players will be playing.

It's a very special day for Nathan, Samuel, Chloé, and Alisha. Together with some other children, they have been invited to show their skills on the middle Saturday of the famous two-week tennis championships at Wimbledon. About 40,000 people come to the tournament on this Saturday to watch the best players in the world compete.

Getting ready

The junior players line up, eager to show off their skills. Samuel practices his serving action, and Nathan goes for a warm-up run around the court to try to stop feeling nervous. Some of the Wimbledon staff help the children with their warm-up.

In this warm-up game, the children have to run through the legs of one member of the staff, then run to hit a high-five with another, before sprinting back to the baseline.

Nathan enjoys playing tennis in front of so many people and hits some great strokes. He is more determined than ever to become a professional player.

Nathan and Alisha have really enjoyed themselves and can't wait to be invited back again. For now, they have packed their tennis rackets in their bags and can wander around the courts to see some other matches being played.

Taking a break

Nathan and Samuel take a well-earned break. They have brought lots of water with them to drink and wear their hats to protect themselves from the blazing sun.

"It's great to be here!"
Alisha

Ida, Helen, and Maria can't wait to go through the royal entrance to the clubhouse. They feel very lucky to see inside.

Tour of Wimbledon

A dream come true! The squad is given a special guided tour of the most famous tennis club in the world. They imagine the cheers of the crowd as they sit at No. 1 Court, where their tennis heroes have won and lost matches.

The trophies

In the clubhouse, the team sees the trophies. The Men's Singles Championship started in 1877, more than 125 years ago. The famous trophy was first presented to the winner in 1887. The Ladies' Singles started in 1884.

The girls look up at the silver plate that is the Ladies' Singles Trophy and dream of winning it. Who knows—maybe one day, one of their names will be engraved on the plate!

The courts

From a balcony, the children get a bird's-eye view of the courts and can watch lots of different matches being played. There are 19 championship grass courts, including Center Court and No. 1 Court, where the most important matches are played. In addition, there are 22 practice grass courts.

Yummy! The strawberries are delicious. During the Wimbledon Championships, about 60,000 lb (27,000 kg) of strawberries are eaten by hungry spectators!

" One day I want to play here! "
Maria

Glossary

B

Baseline—the white line at each end of the court, behind which you serve.

C

Center mark—this is a small line that marks the middle of the baseline.

Court—the rectangular area, marked out by white lines, where tennis is played. A doubles court is 36 ft (10.97 m) wide by 78 ft (23.77 m) long. A singles court is 27 ft (8.23 m) wide.

D

Doubles—a tennis match played with a partner against two opponents.

F

Follow-through—the swing of the racket after you have hit the ball.

G

Groundstroke—a stroke that is used to hit the ball after it has bounced once.

N

Net—the net crosses the middle of the court from one side to the other. The height of the net at the center should be 3 ft (0.91 m).

O

Open-stance—a position you stand in when you are stretching to reach a ball.

P

Professional—a professional tennis player plays tennis for a living.

R

Rally—hitting the ball from player to player for some time without the ball going into the net.

Ready position—the position you stand in when you are waiting to hit the ball.

S

Scoring—in a full game of tennis, a player must win four points to win a game. The points start at 0 (love), then 15, 30, 40, and game. If both players have 40 points (deuce), then the game continues until one player wins by two clear points (advantage point and game point). The first person to win six games wins the set, but the winner must be at least two games ahead. The winner is the player who wins the best of three sets. In some top events, men play the best of five sets.

Service box—the two rectangles that are marked out next to each other on the court on either side of the net. You must serve into your opponent's service box.

Singles—a game of tennis played on your own against a single opponent.

T

Take-back—the action of taking back the racket to hit a stroke.

Index

Acknowledgments

Dorling Kindersley would like to thank the following for their help in the preparation and production of this book:

The All England Lawn Tennis Club, Church Road, Wimbledon, London SW19 5AE, UK (www.wimbledon.org) for their invaluable assistance. Besides staging The Wimbledon Championships, the All England Lawn Tennis Club also introduces tennis to local children through the Wimbledon Junior Tennis Initiative. The photographs in this book are of young players from the Initiative. More than 4,000 young people between the ages of 3½ and 14 have so far benefited from free coaching at the All England Lawn Tennis Club.

If you would like to find out more about learning to play tennis, contact the Lawn Tennis Association at: www.lta.org.uk

Special thanks to Julian Tatum of the All England Lawn Tennis Club for his help and to Dan Bloxham (Head Coach, Wimbledon Junior Tennis Initiative) for acting as consultant; also to the players: Alisha, Chloé, Elizabeth, Helen, Ida, Meg, Nathan, and Samuel, who were fantastic at the photo shoot; thanks also to the parents of all the children, for their time, help, and patience at the photo shoot; and Lisa Lanzarini for directing and styling the photo shoot.